# Lessons of an Opening Heart

THRIVING AFTER OPEN-HEART
SURGERY

## Barbara H. McNeely

*Porcchetta*
PUBLISHING
*SAN ANTONIO, TEXAS*

Porcchetta Publishing
P.O. 591003
San Antonio, TX 78259-1003
www.Porcchetta.com

Disclaimer: The content in this book is not intended as a substitute for medical or professional advice. Readers are encouraged to consult their physician on all health matters, especially symptoms that may require professional diagnosis or medical attention.

Book Editing by Jan Ware Russell PhD contact: 937-303-6849

Quote from "A Trip Around the Sun" by Mark Batterson, Richard Foth, and Susanna Both Aughtmon, © 2015 by Mark Batterson, Richard Foth, and Susanna Both Aughtmon. Baker Books. Used by permission.

Lessons of an Opening Heart / Barbara H. McNeely. -- 1st ed.
ISBN 978-0-9981639-1-8

# Contents

*To my husband, Dick McNeely. Without him, I might not have been here to write this book.*

*Life can only be understood backwards; but it must be lived forwards.*

—Søren Kierkegaard

# And So It Begins

FRIDAY, MAY 22ND, 2015: My alarm clock goes off at the unthinkable hour of 4:00 AM. Once I've showered, there isn't much to do but wait on my husband. While I am waiting the only thing I can do is think. Suddenly, it all becomes too real to me. Until now, it had all been theoretical. The moment facing me becomes so scary.

While I wait, I play Mannheim Steamroller's "Come Home to the Sea" on repeat. This instrumental song always has a calming and centering effect on me. I certainly need that now! Earlier in the week, Magic DeeJay (the music I hear in my head) was playing "I Will Survive" over and over. Appropriately, playing in my head last night was Elton John's "Someone Saved My Life

Tonight." This morning there is no music and there's so much silence to be filled! Everything is silent...no music, no thoughts, no words.

By 5 AM, we are in the car. It's a short drive at this time of day, yet it seems an eternity. To fill the silence, I play Dave Brubeck's "Take Five" on repeat - another song without words.

Too soon, we arrive at our destination. I'm whisked off to room number three, told to remove everything, and an IV is started. They take blood to check my blood type. This was done in a pre-op checkup earlier in the week, but they want to be sure. I'm okay with this since there's a 40 percent chance that I'll need blood. I have now surrendered control of my body to the staff at the hospital - at least until I am out of ICU (intensive care unit).

There's a white board in my room with a sign above it that says, "Welcome to Outpatient Surgery." I find that funny since I think of outpatient surgery as the type where you go home the same day. I have been told that I will be here for anywhere from three to seven days. A nurse explains that outpatient surgery is a term for any individual not already in the hospital's care.

Soon I am wheeled out of room number three and down several halls to a holding room that feels more like a storage area. My husband and I are the only ones there until my surgeon, Dr. R, arrives. She asks if we have questions. There are no questions left to ask. I have asked enough already. I know my condition is severe and that the success rate is 97 percent. I am ready to get started, anxious to be on the other side of surgery, and on the long six to 12 month road to recovery. Dr. R says, "Ready to pray?" We all hold hands as she prays for strength for me, my husband, and for all of the staff.

She leaves and a nurse arrives with the "margarita." That is the last lucid moment I have until Monday.

~♥~

My memories of the next few days are like a dream. I am taken to ICU after surgery where I stay from Friday afternoon until Sunday evening. I cannot sort out what was real from what I dreamed or imagined. I know there had to be more than one nurse during that time, yet all I can recall is one male nurse.

It seems I am in a large room that could accommodate several patients, yet I am here alone. There are large windows at the end of the room. Saturday night there is a strong thunderstorm. I only know it was Saturday from conversations I had much later after I left ICU.

I started to have many strange perceptions. For some reason, I thought that my bed was low to the floor, but apparently it wasn't. At some point, I was convinced there was nothing wrong with me and that I had neither needed nor had surgery, so I decided to leave. I was being held against my will and I was going home! I was tethered to several machines by IVs and tubes. I honestly don't know nor do I want to know about all of the tubes.

However, Sunday afternoon came and they decided to kick me out of ICU, removing lots of tubes and catheters. That's when it seemed like the nurse was being mean to me. I may not have been the best patient at that point. I don't know what drugs they gave me during those first few days, but I do know they were powerful and they continued to mess with my mind long after I was released from the hospital!

~❤~

That Sunday afternoon I moved from ICU to the cardiac unit. My mind was still very foggy. The fog did dissipate a bit every day, but continued all week long. As soon as I got to my room I was given a large, red, heart-shaped pillow. Its purpose, when held tightly to the chest, is to soften the pain of coughs, sneezes, laughter, and even bumps in the road while in a car. This pillow will be my constant companion for the next five or six weeks.

That same night they showed me how to get into bed without (much) pain. You do this by lying on your side and then rolling. No instruction was given for how to get out of bed. In the hospital they had rails to grab, while at home it would be another story.

It's amazing that I remember any of this. I was very groggy and still in quite a fog. I tried to watch television that night, but I kept losing the channel. I think I may have even accidentally called the nurse.

I did fall asleep, but awoke at some point in the night trying to crawl my way out of bed.

I was going home. I had had enough of this place. It took me a little longer to wake up and realize I had no clothes, no ID, no money, and no house keys.

## The Ants Go Marching

Sunday evening also was when the ants showed up. They were crawling everywhere. Not just in a line, but they covered every surface. All of them marching around. Tiny black ants. Ants on the walls. Ants on the baseboards. Ants on the floor. They moved in a coordinated fashion and their lines never crossed. It was funny that my husband couldn't see them.

The ants were still there the next morning when my surgeon came by. They were even crawling on some invisible surface in mid-air. Dr. R put her hands on them! I thought about telling her, but I knew on some level there really were no ants and Dr. R just might think I was crazy.

I thought perhaps they were part of a long-lasting optical migraine. I had been getting optical migraines for about a year, but I had never seen ants and the episodes never lasted more than 20 minutes.

I have since read "Quantum Healing" by Deepak Chopra. Chopra talks about open-heart surgery patients and the fact that some of them have psychotic breaks and begin hallucinating. Some think that little green men are marching up and down the sheets. Chopra suggests that the heart itself may be hallucinating. The trauma of the surgery causes the heart to think reality has changed. It's an interesting theory. And who knows? At any rate, the ants were gone on Tuesday, much to my relief.

Wednesday I was released from the hospital with a long list of instructions and a pile of prescriptions to be filled. Have you ever checked out of a hospital or been with someone checking out? It seemed like there were reams of papers and countless people to sign off on things. It was all very tiring to me. I suspect that everyone needed to have a hand in it so they could bill the insurance company. All I knew was I wasn't paying by that time. I had reached my annual out-of-pocket maximum on the morning of my surgery!

Did I need a walker? Did I need home health care? Did I have all of the prescriptions? Did I have all the home instructions? In total it took us about 5 hours to get all the paperwork together and get home. The drive was only 20 minutes, it was long after 5 PM when we got home, and I was exhausted. Oops! We were supposed to call the hospital in the evening after I got home. Think it's too late to make that call? They should have sent home dinner too! Scratch that, the hospital food was mostly inedible. Wouldn't you think a better quality of food would be offered to people who are healing?

That first night home, I wouldn't even consider tackling the stairs. We slept on the sofa bed downstairs. Except, I think I spent most of the night in the recliner. There are so many things for which no one can prepare you. I had no idea that it was going to be difficult to sleep flat in a bed.

I was on a number of medications when I left the hospital: Iron, Lasix, and potassium. The potassium actually was necessary to replace the potassium the Lasix removed from my body. These medications were temporary. The body has such a delicate balance and medications really mess with that. My extreme sensitivity to chemicals makes it that much harder to be on so many medications. I vowed early on that I would be rid of most of them in very short order.

I was also on Warfarin when I left the hospital. Warfarin is the generic name for the blood thinner commonly known as Coumadin. Coumadin is actually a rat poison! Did you know that? It's an anticoagulant and in large enough doses causes internal bleeding. Fortunately, the dosage is carefully monitored in humans, which means frequent blood tests. This is when I learn why I need that home health care. Since I can't drive for six weeks, someone would have to take off work to take me to have the blood work done.

# Making Other Plans ...

HAVING THE SURGERY WASN'T really the beginning of this journey. It's hard to say when it truly began.

Was the beginning when the right knee started hurting? That was September of 2014. Sometimes I could barely walk and at that time I loathed the stairs in our home. I saw everyone about my right knee. I saw everyone except a medical doctor. I saw more than one chiropractor. I did acupuncture. I had massages. I sought natural supplements. Eventually the right knee pain cleared up.

However, nearly overnight, the left knee began hurting. Only this time it felt different. Immediately, I made an appointment with a doctor. That's why I credit my knees with saving my life. More accurately, it was God who saved my life. I had been getting gentle hints that I should have my health checked and that I needed to find a primary care doctor.

I only ever saw the doctor's PA (Physician Assistant), not the doctor himself. The PA ordered x-rays and an MRI for the knee. The PA also noticed my blood pressure was elevated and heard a heart murmur. The heart murmur did not surprise me because over the years I had been told I had a heart murmur or mitral valve prolapse. What the PA heard was different. She heard it on more than one visit, and so did others. She said it sounded "funny" and suggested that I see a cardiologist to have it checked out.

So I did. The cardiologist ran an EKG (electrocardiogram), listened to my heart, and ordered a number of tests. The results were in after calcium scoring, a stress test, ECHO (echocardiogram), and a CT (computerized tomography) angiogram to rule out an aneurysm. Just three short weeks after the first visit to the cardiologist, my husband and I were told the news: my aortic valve was not functioning properly. It's opening was 75% closed. Yikes! And my heart was working harder to pump blood through, but the volume was greatly reduced. In medical terms it's called Aortic Stenosis. In practical terms it means replacing the aortic valve. In realistic terms it means open-heart surgery.

Even the knees weren't the real beginning. My cardiologist listed these symptoms of Aortic Stenosis: shortness of breath, chest pain, dizziness, passing out, and feet swelling. In fact, I had seen some swelling in my feet off and on for several years. Now I understood that it was something that should have garnered more attention. Perhaps that is what Søren Kierkegaard meant when he said: "Life can only be understood backwards; but it must be lived forwards."

Looking back, it seems like a dream now. Or was it more of a nightmare? There are scars to show that it all happened, but it still seems like an impossibility that this journey happened to me. It all happened so fast! There were just five weeks between my first cardiologist appointment and my surgery.

Everything changed. All my plans went on hold. I missed my Toastmasters Club's meetings. I had to stop the physical therapy for my knees. Soon my life had a single focus: preparing for open-heart surgery and the following recuperation that began as soon as I got out of ICU and continued for months.

That's how quickly it happened. I was busy making plans for my life after my knees healed and it all stopped, because life happened. And isn't that usually how it goes? You're living your life, making your plans, thinking that you're in control. Then, suddenly you or a family member gets sick and for a while, that illness is your life. All your plans are put on hold. Once the crisis is passed, you pick up your life where it left off. You may have missed some events, but your life is relatively unchanged. While you're dealing with the immediacy of the illness or loss, your focus is only on that one event. Your plans are on hold. Yet, once the crisis has passed, you pick up those plans and your life continues as it was before the crisis.

Sometimes though, when you're busy living your life and making your plans, a life event can happen that will forever change the trajectory of your life. Major events like loss of a spouse or child, divorce, or a personal illness or injury can change the course of your life. A personal example was my sister's battle with cancer. Near the end of her fight, nothing else mattered. Afterwards, my world was forever changed. Another example is when my 83-year-old father broke his hip. For months my father was my primary focus. Later I was executor of his estate. After each life event I emerged on the other side a different person.

That is my story. How a visit to the doctor for a sore knee altered the course of my life forever.

Let me tell you about some of the things I learned during this journey.

# Healing

I NORMALLY PAY ALL the bills in our house. The day after I got home from surgery I attempted to pay bills. I pay them all online and it's usually a 20-minute process. I worked for two hours and never paid a single bill. My brain was moving slowly, my hands were weak, and I could not concentrate. I finally had to postpone the bills to another day.

That was when I realized just what a shock surgery had been to my system. When I first learned of my surgery, I went online to find out more about it and how it was done. I wanted to know and at the same time I didn't want to know. One of the early steps in the surgery involves stopping the heart and lungs and putting the patient on a bypass machine. A bypass machine does the work normally done by the heart and lungs. That's when I stopped reading. That was enough. Maybe I didn't want to know. Over the coming weeks as I continued to research, I learned that open-heart surgery is a major trauma that impacts every part of the body.

Healing takes work. It takes a lot of work! Learning to accept that was a huge lesson for me. Everything I did took longer. A shower could take an hour. An outing resulted in exhaustion. The surgery didn't stop me; it just slowed me down.

I learned to applaud the baby steps. Each new development of my recovery - including the progress of me being able to walk three houses up our street up hill - was applauded. Next, it was five houses and then eight. Eventually I was able to celebrate the fact that I could go to lunch and eventually do some shopping. I was always exhausted afterwards. However, it was always better than what I could do the week before.

A lot of work was going on inside me. Feeling tired or even exhausted was to be expected. I learned to embrace rest and naps.

~ ❤ ~

Healing is a process, especially after major surgery. My cardiologist first said that recovery would take three to six months. Then she admitted that full 100% recovery was closer to a year. My surgeon at one point said I would be feeling better at two to three months. Then she changed her mind and said two months.

It was hard to judge my progress when given so many different answers. What I learned to do was to measure my own progress against how I was the day or week or month before. At first it would change day to day. Sometimes I would go back a step or two from the day before. I learned I had to watch the overall trend. Everyone wanted to tell me where I should be at any given stage, including some medical people. The reality is that healing IS a process and only I (and those close to me) am able to determine my progress. Everyone else was just noise.

~❤~

Here's the part the doctors don't tell you: total healing involves much more than the body. The body knows the mechanics of healing the physical body, but the mind and the spirit need to heal as well.

For several weeks following surgery I felt fragile especially outside of my home. I didn't feel stable or steady on my feet, so I was reluctant to be around a lot of people. Even after I no longer felt fragile, I lacked confidence.

Over time, I felt less fragile as I was able to move about and go out on my own. In fact, I have found that I tend to be less fearful than I used to be. After having open-heart surgery, what is there to fear now?

How does one heal completely? It takes a lot of work. Here are some of the things that I did:

First, cardiac rehab was a major help. The primary goal is to build strength and stamina, and at the same time to rebuild confidence and self-esteem.

Second, I found meditation, along with a class on mindful self-compassion, to be helpful, as well as prayer. I found it crucial to be open to new ideas and different ways of looking at the world. In the midst of a very strange presidential election season, I had to disconnect. I still kept up-to-date with what was going on, but I had to stay away from political topics on social media.

# S.O.B.

I WOULD LOVE TO tell you that my recovery process was all lollipops and sunshine, but there was a dark, bleak period. Undiagnosed anemia was my biggest challenge. The rest of the world continued as normal and I had to sit down and catch my breath after walking every 20 steps.

It started two weeks after surgery. I felt as though I was regressing in my recovery. I couldn't sleep. I was very short of breath. I was anxious. The anxiety all centered around my shortness of breath. I have appropriately shortened and simply call shortness of breath S.O.B. It started while my cardiologist was on vacation. I had to see another doctor in the same practice. He was reluctant to do much to help me other than order tests and recommend I eat potassium rich foods.

A week later I had my follow up appointment with my surgeon. The blood that was drawn the week before had hemolyzed (the breaking down of red blood cells with liberation of hemoglobin). Dr. R heard fluid in the lungs and extended the furosemide (aka Lasix: a diuretic) for another week. That also meant extending the potassium. Lasix works by pulling sodium from the body thereby drawing off fluid. My research showed that it also pulls potassium, magnesium, phosphorous, and thiamin from your body! Yet they only supplement for the potassium.

The S.O.B. continued. Eventually, my doctor took me off most of my medications; thinking that one or more of them was the culprit. Due to a comedy of errors, I dealt with S.O.B. for a month before it was finally diagnosed as anemia. The errors included blood that hemolyzed before getting to the lab and also mislabeled blood vials. That month included one ER visit because I could not catch my breath, an after hours call to the cardiologist office, and numerous trips to the doctor.

It was a miserable time. I was constantly out of breath. I could not sleep anywhere except the recliner. I don't know the science behind it, but when you're coping with S.O.B., it's even harder to breathe if you're lying flat on your back.

Every task was a struggle. I made one trip up the stairs each day - to shower and dress. It was an involved process with lots of breaks and usually took one to two hours to complete. Preparing lunch required several breaks. I had a physical therapy person coming to the house. She encouraged me to walk, somehow thinking I could build up to breathing more. That wasn't helpful.

It can be depressing to cope with S.O.B. when you're used to moving fast. The S.O.B. was the worst part of my recovery. The pain from surgery was both expected and controllable. It took much longer than it should have to figure out that anemia was the underlying cause of S.O.B. It should have been obvious. You lose a good bit of blood during open-heart surgery. I was given one unit of packed red blood cells while in the hospital, but that clearly wasn't enough.

There were many tests run during that time. X-rays to look for fluid on the lungs, tests to check for an embolism, even an ECHO to ensure that the new valve was working properly. That was scary. The last thing I needed to think about was the possibility of starting over and repeating surgery!

Eventually, once the blood work showed anemia, my shortness of breath resolved fairly quickly. Soon I was able to walk enough that doing laps in the house was getting old. It seems to be a good recovery sign when you're getting bored.

# Conquering Stairs

STAIRS, YOU EITHER LOVE them or hate them. As a teenager, I loved them. I could get up the stairs two and sometimes three steps at a time. On the day we first looked at our current house with our realtor, another realtor stopped by. She had clients in the car and she had just one question, "Was the master bedroom downstairs?" She left when she was told "No." Looking back, I consider that short conversation an omen.

The stairs in our house are built in three parts. There are seven steps from the ground floor to the first landing. Then there is a right turn and three steps to the second landing, followed by another right turn. From the second landing it's another six steps to the second floor, for a grand total of 16 steps!

I wasn't always so intimate with our stairs. My affair with our stairs started in 2014 with knee problems. When every step is painful, you tend to avoid stairs. Perhaps that is why one of the first questions I asked my cardiologist was how I would manage stairs. I'm sure she thought I was crazy, and she may have been right. However, it seemed a logical question to me. I watched my father recover from a similar surgery. While he didn't have a two story house, he had difficulty with any incline or step. I needed to know if I was going to be able to maneuver the stairs or be consigned to sleeping on the couch. No stairs also meant no shower for a month or two.

As it turns out, climbing stairs with shortness of breath is harder than climbing with painful knees. The first time I went upstairs after my surgery, I climbed all sixteen steps at one time. That was a bad idea and I just barely made it. I was gasping for breath at the top of the stairs and it took ten minutes to recover.

After that experience, my husband placed a folding chair on each of the stair landings so I could take the stairs in phases instead of all at once. On each landing I could rest on a chair. Still, I limited my trips on the stairs. For the first few weeks following surgery, I went upstairs one or two times a day – at most. During the times that I attempted sleeping in our bed, I would make two trips per day. The trips included once after breakfast to shower and dress and the second at bedtime. However, for more than a month, I slept in the recliner downstairs so that I only had to climb the stairs once a day to shower and dress.

I developed a routine to manage the stairs, shower, and dress. At first all three were arduous tasks. I had a shopping bag that was always close at hand. It contained essential items I needed with me at all times. All of which, together, weighed under my allowed 5-pound limit, including the current book I was reading. I would head up the stairs with my shopping bag and my heart pillow.

I would begin up the first set of stairs to that first landing, counting out loud "One, two, three, four, five, six, seven." I would then turn the corner and three more steps "Eight, nine, ten." One of the physical therapists had suggested counting out loud because she believed my shortness of breath was caused by not breathing. This wasn't the source of my problem, but still I counted the stairs out loud.

At the second landing, I would stop and sit in the folding chair. I set my phone's timer for five minutes and would read for at least that long. Almost always, I had my girl cat, Nancy, with me. She followed me quite a bit during those first weeks after surgery. When time was up, I would make it up the last six steps. I would finally make it into the bedroom where I would need to sit for another few minutes.

It could take me ten or fifteen minutes just to get to the shower. From there, everything was an effort and standing was not much of an option. Hence, there was a shower stool that got a lot of use. Time rarely mattered. Unless a home health person was due or I had a doctor appointment, I had all day with not much to do but heal.

During this time of my recovery, I had to work hard at being positive. Everything took effort. Each day seemed to stretch out to double its length. No one could tell me for sure when it would end. I saw my surgeon six weeks after surgery. She told me I would begin to feel better at two months. I was doubtful, but it turned out she was correct. Shortly after the two month mark, I was climbing the stairs five and six times a day fairly regularly. And by 4 1/2 months, I didn't give the stairs much thought.

# Emotions

My surgeon gave me a two-page handout of instructions for the period before surgery. One instruction, to be started one month prior to surgery, read as follows: "As much as possible decrease your exposure to stress and negative situations, even movies. That has been shown to increase spasms of the vessels/arteries."

In truth, I found that I had been disconnecting from stressful situations naturally. Once I knew, in early May, that I was to have surgery, decreasing stress became my number one priority. Thoughts of work in any form went on the back burner. I am a bit of a news and talk radio junkie, but I found myself disconnecting from all of it. For the first month or two following surgery, I avoided most of the news. I knew my own body and that listening to news could agitate it. That was definitely not what I needed.

In reality, worry, fear, and stress do not serve us well. I seem to always be working to rid my life of these negative emotions.

My husband and I saw the movie "Bridge of Spies" about five months after surgery. It was a good movie about a man named Rudolf Abel. He was a KGB undercover agent in North America for a period of time following World War II. Several times in the movie he was in impossible situations. An example is when he was on trial for crimes against the US and his life was hanging in the balance. Each time, people would ask him if he was worried. And each time, he shrugged off the question saying that worry would not help.

I try to remember his response each time I start to worry about things.

Stress is the body's reaction to a threat or a perceived threat. Our mind is what perceives the threat, but it is the body that is affected. During a stress response the body is affected in several ways: adrenaline and hormones are released, heart rate increases, breathing speeds up, blood pressure rises, muscles tense, the nervous system is activated, senses are sharpened, blood sugar rises, and blood clots more easily. These are all good things when there is a real threat or danger. We experience acute stress resulting in the release of adrenaline and the fight or flight reaction. Once the danger passes, we experience a relaxation response.

With chronic stress, our bodies have all of the same reactions, except that cortisol (steroid hormone that regulates carbohydrate metabolism, the immune system, and maintains blood pressure) is released. And with chronic stress, there is no relaxation response at the end. Our fight or flight response is always on. Just looking at the list explains a lot of our 21st century illnesses: blood pressure rises, heart rate increases, hormones are released, and blood sugar rises.

Prior to the 2016 presidential election, I had a number of friends who were constantly posting on Facebook everything negative they saw about the opposing candidate to the one of their choice. Many of these people were posting without checking the truth of their posts. I had to unfollow most of them because I didn't want that stress in my life. The political stress took its toll as a couple of those same friends were eventually hospitalized with heart issues.

# For Girls Only

NOW I'M GOING TO talk about breasts and how they can hinder the healing process. This section is for the girls, the guys who have ample breast tissue, and all the fathers, brothers, and husbands who may have never realized the dilemma associated with breasts.

Bras became a huge problem for me after surgery. My rib cage was very tender. Any bra that was tight would make the ribs ache. For me they all seemed tight. The nurse at my cardiologist's office suggested that I get a good, supportive sports bra. There were a couple of problems with this suggestion. First, many bras have to be put on over the head, which is a real struggle when you have sore ribs and a five inch incision! Second, they tend to be real tight.

Most of the suggestions I got were from people with no experience with open-heart surgery. I struggled for the first four or five weeks. I tried front hook bras, I tried camisoles with built in bras, and they all hurt.

The solution to my dilemma, so it would seem, would be to go bra-less. That brings its own troubles because then your breasts are constantly pulling on the incision making it hurt and slowing healing. The incision then can open and potentially introduce infection.

Still, I admit going bra-less for the first five weeks or so. Going bra-less severely limited my wardrobe. That was ok since I didn't get out much during those early days after the surgery. Many, if not most, days, I would start off wearing a bra but would have to take it off after a couple of hours.

And then, it just seemed to get better. I don't remember exactly when. But, eventually I noticed that I could wear a bra for much longer. Until one day, between seven and eight weeks, I just began wearing a bra all day long.

I also need to mention the yeast infection that I acquired. I noticed its symptoms a day or two after coming home from the hospital. It wasn't a surprise considering all the antibiotics I was given at the hospital. I was thankful that now yeast infection treatments can be purchased over the counter.

# Stuff Happens

HAVE YOU EVER NOTICED that you never just have one health issue? That's me sometimes, and especially in the first part of 2015. I started with knee issues and by May I had a laundry list of medical issues, many requiring a specialist. It is a rare specialist who considers the whole body in their treatment. The cardiologist treats a heart. The orthopedist treats a knee. The ophthalmologist treats eyes, and on and on. By May of 2015 I had the need of an orthopedist, a cardiologist, a rheumatologist, and an ophthalmologist. I also was in desperate need of a primary care doctor who would oversee everything. Here's how it all went down.

In February of 2015, my ophthalmologist determined that I had something called close angle glaucoma. This is not what most people mean when they speak of glaucoma. This condition can result in a rapid increase in pressure and quickly become an emergency situation. March took me to the first orthopedist for my knees. This then led me to a cardiologist in April. Early May brought the aortic stenosis diagnosis, yet it also brought the news about a nodule on my thyroid.

All specialists have their questions and they tend to interpret the answers through the lens of their specialty. Changes in weight or hair loss might indicate a more serious thyroid issue, but each of those occurrences is almost expected following major surgery. However, try telling a specialist that.

There is one other health issue that I have had since age 16. It started as a single perfume that gave me a migraine. Today, it includes all perfumes, fragrances, as well as vehicle exhaust, airplane fuel, most commercial cleaners, and a lot more. Basically, I react to many chemicals and that becomes a problem in our world that is so full of chemicals. In 2015, I found I needed to add many medications to the list of chemicals to avoid. I even reacted to medications I had taken in the past.

As a result, I was eventually taken off all medications. I have never been fond of taking medications, which may explain my aversion to doctors. We seem to live in a society where every illness or ache or pain we have requires a prescription to fix it. I prefer a more natural approach through the power of the foods that I eat, and the foods I choose to avoid.

# The Amazing
# Human Body

THE HUMAN BODY IS amazing! Science defines
processes that occur within the body, yet isn't
it just short of miraculous that it all works like
it does? Take healing as an example. Here's the
condensed version of my surgery: They made
a five-inch incision, cut through the sternum
- (a narrow bone running down and connect-
ing the ribs), stopped my heart and lungs using
cardiopulmonary bypass to take over blood oxy-
genation and circulation. The surgeon spread
the ribcage, cut through the pericardium, and
cut open my heart. She then removed the aortic valve and replaced it with a valve from a pig,
sewed up the heart, and did a couple of bypasses
- you know, because they were there! The pro-

cess then ended by the restarting of my heart, removing the bypass machine, wiring the sternum back together, and then using some kind of awesome, magical glue to close up the incision!

That's when the real work begins. The body calls out the troops to heal and mend the cuts, tears, and bones. The sternum was just one of the bones damaged. The ribs had tiny cracks all the way around, a result of being spread to create an opening. My surgeon told me that the pericardium (the membrane surrounding the heart) is cut open during surgery and is never stitched back together.

I think healing in general is just this side of miraculous. Armies of cells are called to the scene for a simple cut. At a level most don't understand, our bodies know how to heal from the simplest cut all the way to open-heart surgery.

Modern medicine is also pretty amazing. This type of surgery previously required a ten to twelve inch incision. The large incision was either stitched or stapled closed. That procedure explains why they were often referred to as zippers. It's mind-boggling to me that modern medicine uses a type of glue to hold an incision together. Each hole of the zipper method made by a stitch or a staple was an invitation to infection. So, thank God for the glue.

Aside from the healing process itself, there were other lessons to be learned. While my surgery was concerned with the heart, my entire body was impacted. Knowing that all parts of our body are interconnected shouldn't be surprising. Surgery had crazy effects on me.

I typically sneeze at least once per day, every day, every season. It's just what I do. Not that I plan it or bring it on, it just happens.

Following open-heart surgery, those tiny cracks in the ribs are sensitive to pressure and movement. They are sensitive to any movement. Movements including coughing, laughing, bumps in the road, and especially sneezing. That's what the heart pillow is for. Holding that pillow tight will lessen the pain of coughs, laughs, etc.

Sneezes are in their own class because they often appear without warning. Somehow, my body knew to suppress sneezes. I did not sneeze for the first five weeks following surgery. Those first sneezes **were** painful when they returned.

This story isn't about sneezing. It's about the amazing ways our bodies can adapt and accommodate on levels we don't even think about or understand.

Infection following surgery happens and it can be scary. My father had an infection after neck surgery. He was on intravenous (IV) antibiotics for a couple of months. Infection was one thing I watched out for. And it's why I used the antiseptic soap given to me by the hospital, in spite of the fact that it had a fragrance I could not stand.

Even so, five or six weeks following surgery, I noticed signs of infection along my incision. It turned out to be a superficial skin infection and not a serious issue.

My hairdresser, Cindy, taught me that major surgery impacts hair. She has seen its effect on many of her clients. Cindy has been cutting my hair since 2002. In some ways, she knows it better than I do. It was in December of 2015, seven months after surgery, that she mentioned there was a lot of new growth in my hair. She told me she had been waiting to see how surgery would affect my hair. She had seen it often enough. She has seen hair loss, curly hair turn straight, and straight hair turn curly. Even today, there are still changes in the way my hair curls. More evidence that open-heart surgery is a trauma for the entire body - including the hair on the head.

The weirdest change in my body, by far, was in the area of my armpits. I never imagined anything quite like this. A few days after surgery, I noticed that they were red and itchy. This was followed by peeling and pain. After six weeks or so, they were just red and sometimes painful - especially when applying deodorant.

While we were on vacation in New Mexico, my armpits were in such a mess that I stopped using deodorant. I said I would stop for a day or two or until the odor became too much. The strange thing is that there was no odor.

Do you know people who don't have to wear deodorant? Not the ones that you wish would. I'm talking about the people who actually don't need it. Don't you hate them? Plus, some of them attribute it to being vegan, vegetarian, or holier-than-thou in some way. Let me just state up front that I am NOT one of those people. I have always **needed** to wear deodorant. Often I did not have one that was effective enough.

That is why I was surprised when I could not detect an odor that first day I went without. That was October, 2015. I went without deodorant until March or April of the next year. Even now, the odor is much less than it used to be.

Isn't it curious that having open-heart surgery could affect body odor? I can't explain it so I just leave it as a mystery.

# Helpful Things

MY SISTER SPENT MONTHS in and out of the hospital after she developed lung cancer. She had several small notebooks with her. She used them to track medications, doctor visits, blood pressure, etc. I liked her idea of keeping notes but decided to keep all of mine in one notebook as I faced open-heart surgery.

I started my journal a couple of weeks before surgery. I used it to track information from doctors, hospitals and labs. I recorded questions that I had and I carried it with me to all doctor appointments. It was with me in the hospital and was referenced by my husband and my surgeon. In fact my surgeon even made some notes for me in the hospital.

It started out as a brand new black composition book and was my faithful companion during those first few weeks following surgery. Over time it became worn and scratched up. It came in real handy more than once for tracking medication changes. I would also record blood pressure readings, weight, physical activity, test results and questions for the next doctor visit.

It's more than a cliché to say that laughter is the best medicine. It was especially helpful for me to remember to laugh and have fun. Sometimes I would sit and sing just for the fun of it. Funny movies were also a good idea. That was even advised by my surgeon. At one of my visits to her office, she suggested going to the movies and having fun. She even suggested that we go see "Minions." We did and loved it.

I have never been accused of being vain. I do take pride in looking good, but I don't always measure up to other people's standards. I'm not the girl that has to have on makeup to go out in public. In fact, because of allergies, I have quit wearing makeup entirely. Open-heart surgery and knee issues have been very humbling.

I used a cane for several weeks before surgery, because my left knee needed extra support. Bonus: I found that people are more willing to open doors for you! Once or twice I even used the motorized scooters in the grocery store. I frequently used them after surgery because it wasn't optional. My choices were to use the scooter or not go to the store.

Perhaps the hardest were the days just after surgery when I had to ask for help cutting my food, feeding myself, and other tasks we all take for granted.

You know your world has gotten really small when you're looking forward to a doctor appointment or visit from the home health nurse. My recovery was a long and sometimes rocky experience. It became imperative to have other things on the calendar; a visit, lunch, or coffee with friends helped to break up the monotony. I had to have things to look forward to. I was dreading my birthday. But it turned out to be a good day. I wanted to go to the Holistic Chamber meeting and see friends, but I still couldn't drive. My husband took the day off work. I was able to schedule a badly needed haircut for that day. We ended the day seeing "Inside Out."

# A Real Getaway

On Saturday, October 3rd of 2015, - just 4 1/2 months after my surgery - my husband and I set out on a road trip to Albuquerque, New Mexico. The trip was prompted by a passing conversation with a stranger back in August. The conversation mentioned the Albuquerque International Balloon Fiesta. When the conversation of vacation came up, I suggested the Balloon Fiesta.

We set out in our Explorer with my iPhone-turned-iPod loaded with almost 4,000 songs. We planned our trip route to include seeing different scenery than any previous trips – as much as possible. The first day was all driving – for twelve hours. Thanks to the tunes we had on hand, it was a pleasant drive.

On day 2, we were up super early to go to the International Balloon Fiesta. It's impossible to describe exactly what that was like. We watched hundreds of balloons pop up on the field and then take off into the air. We were able to walk around among the balloons. It was beautiful to watch and to marvel at the carefully organized and orchestrated chaos. If you get the chance, make a trip to the Balloon Fiesta.

My husband and I were fortunate that his daughter, Nina, once lived in Albuquerque. She had many suggestions on things to do and places to eat during our trip. We didn't get to all of them, so another trip is definitely in order.

On day 3 we went to Taos, New Mexico. We drove the High Road to Taos, which is a scenic, winding road through the Sangre de Cristo Mountains. It was a beautiful, scenic drive. We made only one stop on the way, in the town of Chimayo. There we visited El Santuario de Chimayo, which is a Roman Catholic Church and a National Historic Landmark. This shrine is a must see if you're in the area.

When we arrived in Taos, we toured the Taos Pueblo. It was interesting to learn of the culture and history of the area. Nina had suggested that we check out the Rio Grande Gorge Bridge. The bridge is 565 feet above the Rio Grande and is the seventh highest bridge in the U.S. I had to fight my irrational fear of heights in order to walk partway across. The panoramic view was beautiful.

Tuesday, day 4, brought us back to the Balloon Fiesta. On this day we were blessed with sunshine – which made the balloons even more beautiful. The balloons were also able to fly higher, further, and longer than on Sunday. We also drove to Santa Fe where we shopped, ate lunch and visited the Georgia O'Keefe Museum. We randomly ran into a friend from San Antonio, Texas!

**Standing On A Corner**

It may sound crazy, but I have wanted to visit Winslow, Arizona and stand on a corner since 2007 or maybe earlier. I thought I was going to complete that item in 2013, but it didn't quite work out. Our plans for this trip included a visit to Winslow on day 5. There really wasn't that much to see or do in Winslow, except stand on the corner and eat lunch.

On the way back to Albuquerque from Winslow, we stopped at the Acoma Pueblo. This was another recommendation from Nina and she encouraged us to take the tour. Sadly, we got there too late for the last tour of the day. We watched the movie that gave a history of the pueblo. The film and what we could see of the pueblo from a distance has definitely piqued our interest in going back some day soon and taking the tour. Before going to the Acoma Pueblo, we speculated on what differences we might see from one pueblo to the next. Even without the full tour, we learned that the Taos Pueblo and Acoma Pueblo are very different and it's worth seeing both.

**UFOs**

The last 2 days of our trip were mostly driving. We drove Highway 380 from Interstate 25 to Roswell, New Mexico. This was primarily a two-lane road with very few other cars, a few tiny towns, and a lot of hills. It was a very long

150 plus miles that had absolutely no cell phone service most of the way. We stopped in Roswell and visited the Roswell UFO Museum. We did the tour mostly for a laugh.

I definitely need to go back to the Balloon Fiesta. That friend I ran into in Santa Fe had gone up in a balloon. I saw one of her pictures on Facebook and realized that the absolute best balloon shots were from above! When we make that trip, we'll also plan to tour the Acoma Pueblo.

This trip was both recovery therapy and a renewal for me. I have now dubbed it the best vacation ever and cannot figure out why we've never made a trip like that before. But, rest assured, I have plans for other such trips in the future. Perhaps the best part of the trip was that I often felt as though I should pinch myself to be sure it was all real. Most of the time, it was hard to believe that I was the same girl who had undergone open-heart surgery so recently! I even asked my husband at one point, as we walked the entire Balloon Fiesta Park, why he hadn't told me in June and July that I would be making this trip in October! There were times that I could have used that kind of encouragement.

# What I Would Do Differently

WHAT COULD I HAVE done differently to make this journey easier knowing all I know today?

If I could go back far enough, it would be to an incident more than 20 years ago that led me to a cardiologist. He ran many tests and gave a diagnosis of aortic valve thickening or something similar. On the last visit to his office, I saw the doctor and he said he would talk to me when I was done with this one last test. Perhaps he might have told me that what he had found could one day result in the need to replace that valve. His staff insisted that he did not need to see me again. I should have persisted and gained information that might have better prepared me for my diagnosis of aortic stenosis.

I know better than to dwell on thinking about what might have been. It won't change anything and quite likely could lead to insanity. Still, sometimes I wonder.

I also could go back four or five years before surgery. That is when I began experiencing swelling in my feet and ankles as well as occasional shortness of breath. Now I know that together these were indicators of aortic stenosis. Clearly I would have benefited from having a regular primary care doctor during that time.

Another thought not to dwell on, right? So where does that leave me? I have a few ideas on how I could have made the recovery process better.

I was in a dark place for a while, primarily because of my anemia that went undetected for far too long. I have talked with a few people with similar experiences. It seems almost obvious that one could become anemic following major surgery. Yet the doctors missed it for far too long. I'm thinking that I needed someone to be an advocate for me during that time. I certainly had no energy for the task.

Something else I have learned, as a result of the arthritis in my knees, is the healing power of bone broth. When I talk about bone broth, I am talking about beef or chicken bones cooked for 8 hours or more to extract the gelatin from the joints and the trace minerals from the bones. I make that distinction because what you find in a store may say bone broth, but it isn't always made from the bones. If the broth is made just from chicken pieces and no bones, it just isn't the same thing. I now believe that I should have started on bone broth in the weeks leading up to my surgery.

Another thing I would have done differently would have been to have more visitors during my convalescence. It got lonely at times during the day. I'm sure I wasn't the best of company, but more human interaction might have helped that. Mind you, I do love my cats, but they're rather poor conversationalists. Who knows, though, they might say the same about me. If only we had a common language.

# Keep Moving

ON WEDNESDAY, NOVEMBER 4TH, 2015, Magic Deejay was playing "Pomp & Circumstance" in my head when I woke up. You know that song, right? The song they play at graduations? In a sense it was graduation day for me, but not your typical graduation. I dressed in workout clothes, rather than a cap and gown. At the end of my workout, after they took my blood pressure for the final time, I received my certificate of completion from cardiac rehab.

What is cardiac rehab? Cardiac rehabilitation or rehab is a medically supervised program for anyone who has had a heart attack, heart surgery, angioplasty or a stent. The program typically includes exercise and education on heart healthy living. Some programs include counseling to reduce stress. Going into it, I knew very little; except that my cardiologist had recommended that I go.

For me, it was a twelve-week program. Every Monday, Wednesday, and Friday I left home at 6:15 AM to go to Cardiac Rehab. I rode a stationary bike, worked out on the NuStep, used an arm bike, did resistance training, and occasionally walked a treadmill. The staff took blood pressure before, during, and after workouts. I wore a heart monitor while exercising as well. Gradually, they increased the time and intensity of my workouts. There were as many as twelve people in our class. The majority of participants were male, but the age differences were vast. There were people that looked to be 20-30 years old on up to 70-80 year olds. Participants came in all shapes and sizes too.

I was at first reluctant to do the full program. It was a long drive and I wanted to find a place to workout that was closer to home. Eventually, I committed to completing the program and even attended the education day.

Wednesday, November 4th, was my last day. My thirty-sixth visit! Completing the program was a major triumph because I decided I would finish no matter what. My knee pain from osteo-arthritis returned towards the end so I limped into rehab the last four days. But, I finished and got my certificate. I was told not to come back, in the most loving way, of course.

In the end, I thoroughly enjoyed the program. Not only did I build strength and stamina, the emotional support from the team helped to rebuild self-confidence and self-esteem.

Cardiac education was offered at no extra charge as part of cardiac rehab. It was eight hours in a classroom spread over two days. It covered many areas including the heart and heart disease, the importance of exercise, the effects of stress on your heart and relaxation techniques, high blood pressure, diabetes and its impact on the heart, medications, and heart healthy eating.

Our bodies are fine-tuned machines and should be treated that way. Regular exercise, good sleep, reduced stress, control of weight, blood pressure and blood sugar levels were all emphasized in this education program.

I was surprised to learn that cardiac rehab isn't always covered by insurance. There was no cost to me because I had met my out of pocket maximum for the year. Otherwise it was subject to my deductible and copay. That's just one more piece of evidence that our system is really one of sick care rather than health care.

Seriously, if our system truly provided health care we might see our gym membership or yoga classes covered as well as dental care. We know that dental care and a healthy mouth are critical to our overall health, yet so little of dental is covered, if at all. What if our system sponsored health coaching or cooking classes to teach everyone how to eat healthier. I dare say, in the long run, it would be cheaper than prescription medications.

Cardiac rehab is just the beginning. We've all heard how important exercise is. And the rehab program is a sensible way to get started moving. But it does not end there. We all need movement. For the physical benefits as well as the mental benefits. What do they suggest for depression? Movement. What do they suggest for stress or anxiety? Movement. What do they suggest for staying young? Movement.

So it's a matter of finding something you love to do. That way you want to continue. Right now I am doing yoga and riding my stationary bike. I really love the yoga. Most of the time I'm pretty good at making time for the bike. Swimming is what I would love to do.

Mainly, I like to remember this:

Do we stop moving because we get old?

OR, do we get old because we stop moving?

# No Two People

WE ALL REACT DIFFERENTLY to any situation.
We have different expectations and we have different outcomes. I want to share observations
of other people who have had similar surgeries
and how they responded to their surgery.

### Example 1

When I was in college, I took a course titled
"Medical Sociology." "Sociology" because it was
a degree requirement for my degree in Biology.
"Medical" because I found it interesting. We had
an assignment to interview someone with an illness and to write a paper about it. I still have
that paper from college. By the way, I made an
"A-" on it. At some point after my surgery I dug
it out again.

A classmate of mine, I'll call him Paul, was born with a hole between the two lower chambers of his heart, a defective pulmonary valve, and a heart murmur. By the age of seven, Paul had gone through two open-heart surgeries. Following the surgeries, his activities were not severely limited but he always had to watch out for chest pains or shortness of breath. I interviewed Paul, when he was 21. He had recently learned of a defective aortic valve - similar to what I had. His condition was in the early stages and was being monitored.

I lost track of Paul after graduation. When I dug out the paper last year, I decided to search for him online. Sadly, I learned that he had passed away at the age of 47. I am guessing that his death was related to his heart issues, though I do not know for sure. When I read his obituary, it was obvious that he did not let his heart issues stop him. He married and had two children, was a very successful business owner, and a leader in his community.

~♥~

**Example 2**

My father had open-heart surgery to replace
his aortic valve at the age of 79. He spent many
days in ICU, in a room with no windows, and
no connection to the outside world. He was in
a place where he could not tell day from night.
As a result, he went into what doctors call a twi-
light state. He had very strange dreams and hal-
lucinations during that time. When he left the
hospital he had two to three people caring for
him - his wife, stepdaughter and a maid. They
waited on him and kept track of all his medications during his recovery. He made the initial
appointment for cardiac rehab, but he never
went. He believed he knew what was best. So, he
rode his stationary bike at a very slow pace. As a
result, he never seemed to have much stamina
after his surgery.

A few years later, at age 83, he fell and broke
his hip. A body needs all its reserves to heal
from such an injury. Any underlying health
conditions only make it harder. Dad never re-
covered from his broken hip and subsequent
surgeries. At one point his doctor speculated
that he might have undiagnosed COPD (Chron-

ic Obstructive Pulmonary Disease). We'll never know for certain, but I'll always wonder if the outcome would have been different if he had gone through cardiac rehab.

**Example 3**

Recently, I met a man I'll call George. George had gone through surgery similar to mine roughly three months after my surgery. When I met him, he wanted to share his message. He felt his life was spared for a reason and that his time wasn't up. He believed his work on earth was not finished. His message was that it could happen to any of us so we should be seen by a cardiologist at least every 5 years.

He told me that he was glad to be alive, while his entire demeanor said the opposite. He lacked enthusiasm. He lacked a spark, as if he were depressed. In talking further I learned that he had lost a friend shortly after his surgery. Something in his voice told me that he felt some guilt for still being alive while his friend was gone. This is called survivor's guilt, a feeling as if it should have been him.

~❤~

Seven weeks after my surgery, on a visit to my surgeon, my husband and I rode the elevator with a lady who had recently had open-heart surgery. We knew that without asking because she had a red, heart-shaped pillow just like mine. There was a strange connection between us since we had both been through a major life-saving trauma. On that short elevator ride, we showed our scars and compared surgery dates. She was only three weeks out from surgery. My husband observed that our surgery dates were almost like a new birthday. That is true because May 22, 2015 is the day that I got a new chance at living for without that surgery, I might not be here to tell this story.

Mark Batterson, in "A Trip Around the Sun" described his near death experience and how it changed him. The circumstances were different than mine, but as I read about his experience during the summer, shortly after my surgery, I felt as though these words could have been written for me: "But the worst day of my life turned into the best day of my life because I finally discovered that every day is a gift from God."

When I first learned of my need for open-heart surgery, it was scary. Once I was safely past the surgery, I began to see the blessing that it was. Without the ability to have such surgery, I most likely would not be typing these words right now. I was thankful that the problem was found and could be fixed. I wonder just what it is that God has in store for me now.

My intention was always to have the very best outcome following surgery. I followed all of the rules: I kept all the doctor appointments, I did no lifting of anything over 5 pounds for 2 months; I didn't drive for 6 weeks. I was fairly self-sufficient during my recovery. That's just who I am. I've never liked to be dependent on others and I was eager for the day I would be independent again.

I had seen the outcomes of Paul and my dad due to their conditions, and like George, I have a message:

Of course, see your cardiologist. But more than that - Don't accept that you're feeling tired or have low energy as an inevitable result of getting older. It shouldn't be that way. And if you are feeling that way, keep pushing doctors until you find out why. It could save your life!

# Best of Both Worlds

MY LIFE'S JOURNEY HAS led me to a lovely group of holistic practitioners. Some embrace modern Western medicine in addition to more holistic approaches. Others seem to shun "modern" medicine entirely.

For many months, I coped with swelling in my feet, ankles, and legs and blood pressure issues. Sometimes my blood pressure would be close to normal and other times it would be quite high. I talked with holistic people. They had this remedy and that remedy. The nutrition shops would suggest various supplements for blood pressure and others for the swelling. I got all the usual recommendations of elevating my feet and even standing on my head. The doctors tell you to cut back on salt and then prescribe blood pressure medications. In either case, all they are doing is treating symptoms. Blood pressure isn't a disease; it's a symptom of another disease or problem. The same is true of fluid retention that causes swelling in your feet, ankles, and legs, it is a symptom of another problem. Everyone had a suggestion regarding how to manage my symptoms. Yet not one person thought about the fact that there could be something far more serious going on.

I still believe in holistic practices. But, I also believe they should exist in our world as part of a total package - a package that also includes modern medicine. No holistic practitioner ever came along who could detect that my heart had a defective valve. And certainly there was no holistic approach that could have healed the valve. In fact, one of the holistic practitioners I respect freely admits that holistic solutions are not always the answer.

# One Year Later

ON MAY 22ND, 2016, a year to the day after my surgery, Magic DeeJay was playing "Celebration" by Kool and the Gang when I woke up! And it is a most appropriate song. As this day is certainly a cause for celebration. I am celebrating renewed life, and to use a phrase coined by Rachel Naomi Remen, a celebration of "endbeginnings."

In reality, I started celebrating on Friday. I could not have asked for a more perfect weekend. What am I celebrating? It was one year ago this day that I had my open-heart surgery. A life saving surgery that has also been life altering. My husband called that day, May 22nd, 2015, a birthday. It is a one year birthday marking the official end of the healing process. My cardiologist and my surgeon both told me that complete recovery from surgery could take six to twelve months. Each month I have felt better and better. Today I feel much better than I did before the surgery. I'm so thankful for this chance at continued life.

This day of celebration was planned several months back. I planned to have brunch with Crystal, my friend and business coach, to celebrate. We met at 10:30 AM at La Fonda on Main in San Antonio. I chose the location because it is one of my favorite places and their brunches are heavenly. I had Pancakes de Naranja - pancakes with orange sauce. Delicious! It came with scrambled eggs, a spicy cheese sauce, and bacon. For me it isn't Sunday without bacon. It was a lot of food and I ate most of it. I figured it was okay since last year on this date I didn't eat anything. That's 'Barbara Logic' in case you were wondering!

### Endbeginnings

According to Rachel Naomi Remen, there are no endings without beginnings. Hence the term endbeginnings. The end of a year is followed by the beginning of a new year. The end of a normal pregnancy is followed by the beginning of a new life. In fact, the word commencement is used to describe the ceremony where students graduate. Their time in school is ending, but the ceremony's name is a commencement or beginning. And so, for me it is the end of healing and the beginning of the next phase of my life. I am excited for that next phase and also extremely grateful that I live in a time where it is possible to be given this second chance.

I took my book with me to brunch. That's the composition book that I started on May 13th, 2015. It is a record of doctor visits, notes from those visits, and much more. It is a record of progress as well as notes for when things did not progress. For months, it went everywhere I went. In the beginning, each page represented one day since there was so much to write down. Some days required two pages for notes. One measure of progress was when I went from one day per page to two days on each page. Eventually, several days were on each page. Finally, I was feeling so much better that I would forget to write in it at all. In fact, the last entry was made on April 19th, 2016. On the one year anniversary, while we were at brunch, Crystal and I wrote the final page for this book. I thought about having a book burning, but that book holds too much valuable information. It is also a reminder of all that I have gone through and accomplished in this year.

I asked Crystal to write in it first. What she wrote helped me to see just how far I had come:

"Barbara, I am so honored to celebrate this day with you! I am also grateful for this friendship. You are not just a survivor, but a champion. You have come through so much and you continue to learn and persevere. Never can you doubt the strength you have for overcoming any obstacle. I am proud to know you and I know this is just the beginning."

# What's Next?

WHAT IS NEXT FOR me? At this point, the sky should be the limit. There should be nothing to fear. Having faced open-heart surgery and coming out much better on the other side, what is there to fear?

One thing I have learned is that I am always a work in progress. I'm still coping with the knee issues and trying to figure out a way around having knee replacement surgery. If I wait long enough, maybe science will find a better way.

I have learned recently that I am much too stressed out and it's all my own doing. I learned that stress can actually cause me physical pain. I went away for a week in November 2016 to a little bed & breakfast in Pipe Creek, Texas. It is called Bella Green. I stayed in the tiny house for four nights. Mostly I was writing. But, I was also there to recharge and regroup. I had no schedules, no decisions, and nothing commercial! I even avoided all the election night hype.

I noticed while I was gone that my knees hurt much less. The pain was almost not there. Even first thing in the morning I didn't have as much pain and stiffness. I attributed it to the fact that I didn't have a flight of stairs to contend with. That was partially true.

However, within a couple of hours of arriving home, my knees were hurting. I had made two trips up the stairs, so at first I thought it was the stairs. Except that didn't make a lot of sense. It wasn't until a few days later that I realized there was a huge stress component that just may have contributed to the knee pain. Here's how:

I got home and had to unload the car. I wanted to get everything put away. I needed to start laundry and I had to do this and I had to do that. Yet, this was another example of me putting too much on myself. I need to remind myself to be mindful and to take each thing as it comes.

Can stress really bring on pain? I believe it can. The stress response releases hormones that can definitely impact pain.

# An Open Heart

WHEN I WAS FIRST told that I needed open-heart surgery, I reacted calmly. I accepted the reality of the circumstances almost as if I had seen it coming. I reflected back to that one trip to a cardiologist 20 years earlier. Deep down, I suspected there was a problem. I was also thankful that the diagnosis and solution wasn't any worse than it was. I watched my father go through the same surgery several years earlier. He was 79 at the time. I had the advantage of relative youth and overall better health.

At the same time, it seemed inconceivable that it could happen to me. And therein lies the truth. I did not panic right away because I don't think I really believed it was happening to me. The night before surgery and the months of recovery told a different story. Yet, as I write this in February of 2017, it again seems to be incredible that it really was my surgery. Perhaps that is a defense that we use to protect ourselves from dwelling on such things too much.

When I told my friend, Karen, about my upcoming surgery, her response was unexpected. She said, "The quickest way to an open heart is through open-heart surgery." Which started me wondering, "Does my heart need opening?" This is a question that has been on my mind a lot. What did it even mean to have an open heart? Does the fact that I even ask that question mean that my heart does need opening?

It was all an open question that I left to the universe, trusting that answers would come in due time. Eventually, I was led to Elizabeth Gilbert's book, "Eat, Pray, Love." When the book first came out, I was never inspired to read it. Then I saw Liz Gilbert being interviewed for her book "Big Magic" and was intrigued.

That's when I decided to watch "Eat, Pray, Love." I watched it just before the one year anniversary of my surgery, and then knew I had to learn more. That was when I bought and read "Eat, Pray, Love." Like most books, it had much more of her story than the movie. At one point, Richard from Texas told of how he had prayed and prayed for an open heart. He said that he kept begging God to open his heart. And so, his prayer was answered in the form of emergency open-heart surgery. I burst out laughing when I read that. Now I knew why I was drawn to the book.

Recently, I realized how much "in my head" I am. I tend to overthink and over plan everything. It does come in handy, at times. I spend a lot of time planning Thanksgiving dinners. I develop a detailed schedule of what needs to be done and when. The planning starts the weekend before with the shopping and then starting on Monday preparing food for the meal. Thursday is mapped out as a timeline. It works well and everything gets to the table at the right time. But overthinking isn't always good. I can overthink to the point that there is no room for spontaneity.

I realize now that an open heart is a journey, not a single event. Like peeling an onion, more is revealed to me each day. I just have to be open and listen and watch. Recently I have been working with Twyla, a Spiritual Life Coach. She did a soul level reading for me, in which she told me what my Divine Nature and Divine Gift were. This was all new to me and perhaps it is to you also. Your Divine Nature tells your soul level qualities such as your soul level personality and how you are wired. Your Divine Gift is your soul's main energy - your naturally abundant energy. But you have to choose to work with it and it isn't asserted in your life by default.

Not surprising, my Divine nature is technical. I've spent much of my career in technical fields. What did surprise me was that my Divine Gift is love and healing. That's when I realized I had been suppressing my Divine Gift. It **IS** a gift and I need to start using it.

Finally, I realize there are signs everywhere that I now have an open heart. A heart that knows it might be broken again one day, but it is open to the possibilities. Also, on another level, I realize that I had an open heart all along, I just hadn't embraced it.

I'm taking the advice of the medicine man in "Eat, Pray, Love" and looking at the world through my heart instead of my head. I'm excited for where this journey called life will lead me.

# Acknowledge-ments

Writing a book is a solitary exercise that involves many people.

First and foremost, thank you to my husband, Dick, for his love and support during this process.

I am truly grateful to my editor, Jan, for all of her hard work. She started out as my editor, but I'm grateful now to call her my friend. Also, kudos to Jan, and her sister Joy, for their suggestions that made for a beautiful book cover.

I greatly appreciated the work that my proofreaders, Crystal and Jeana, for their suggestions and for catching those last few errors.

And I am really blessed to have Karen, Crystal, Jan, Joy, Jeana, Twyla, and many others as my moral support.

# About the Author

Barbara H. McNeely learned to love science in seventh grade from a teacher whose love of science was contagious. In college, she majored in biology and then worked in research for several years. Her curiosity about health and wellness led her to study more about it. She has been blogging for several years now, primarily on health topics and her own health issues. Little did she know that she would need all of that knowledge for her own health crisis.

Barbara has always loved music and has so many song lyrics in her head that they crowd out important information. Recently, she realized that a word or phrase, either spoken or though, could bring to mind a song lyric using that word or phrase. She now refers to this talent as Magic DeeJay. To learn more about Magic DeeJay, visit Barbara.McNeely.com/MagicDeeJay.

Barbara lives in San Antonio, Texas with her husband, Dick, and her two cats, Ronnie and Nancy. You can find her online at BarbaraMcNeely.com and MariposaNaturals.com.